The Maker's Mark Story

The Maker's Mark Story
From Dream to Major Brand
In Two Generations

Joel Whitaker

WHITAKER & COMPANY, PUBLISHERS, INC.

Set in 12 point Book Antiqua.
ISBN 978-0940195080

WHITAKER & COMPANY, PUBLISHERS, INC.
PO Box 224, Spencerville, MD 20905
www.bevnewsonline.com
www.beveragebarons.com

Table of Contents

Introduction

Although there are other books about Maker's Mark, this is the first written with a tourist in mind.

Distilling is tremendously important to Kentucky, and bourbon is especially so, since Kentucky produces 95% of the world's bourbon. More than 8,600 jobs in Kentucky are connected to the distilling industry, earning more than $413 million a year.

There are more barrels of bourbon aging in Kentucky (4.9 million barrels) than there are people in the Commonwealth (4.3 million).

In these pages, you'll learn how a chance argument in the Samuels' living room led to the creation of Maker's Mark, why there's been only one ceremony at the distillery, how Maker's Mark ceased to be a hobby and became a significant business, and how the only line extension in 50 years was created.

You'll also learn how the day-to-day production is overseen by a woman from the Washington State wine country, how the quality is maintained from year to year, how the bourbon in the bottle today retains the flavor and characteristics of the first batch years ago.

And you'll learn the history of the place, why it's a National Historic Landmark.

You'll see pictures of key people at the distillery as well as some of the historic buildings.

The Maker's Mark Story

While the people at Maker's Mark cooperated in this book by being available for interviews, photos, etc., they exercised no editorial control whatsoever. The work product is solely mine.

I hope you enjoy it.

-- Joel Whitaker

Chapter 1

When Mom Told Dad To Get a Job, Maker's Mark Was Born

"Maker's Mark began in our living room," Bill Samuels Jr. recalled. I had asked him to tell the Maker's Mark story. He continued:

"Mom screwed up her courage and announced to my Dad that he needed to get a job. He had thought in his retirement that he would run our farm.

"But Mom had been running our farm successfully and didn't think she needed his help. So she announced that not only did he need to get a job but he needed to get out of the house and was welcome back at 6 p.m. and not before."

Samuels father had been talking about trying to create a bourbon that didn't have any bitterness. Prodded by Marge Samuels ultimatum, in October 1953, he went down to the Marion County courthouse and bought Burks Spring Distillery for $35,000. He said it was the biggest check he had ever written.

He went to his best friend, who was president of the bank, and asked him to serve on the board and he said yes.

He then went to him as a board member and said he would like to borrow some money, and the banker said no. "There's no future for bourbon. It's been going down for the last five years, and the public has decided it likes the more sophisticated imported products," the banker said.

At that point, Bill Samuels' dream went from being a business to being a hobby, and it stayed a hobby for about 14 years. Because it did, it allowed him to gear back expectations, to work on the craft, not to get in too big a hurry and not to get over-leveraged financially.

Help from Other Distillers

Samuels' best friends were other distillers. "On many Saturdays we walked next door to visit the Beams. In fact, Col. Jim Beam was my Godfather until he died in 1947. Ed Shapira, founder of the Heaven Hill Distillery, lived nearby, and Pappy Van Winkle lived not too far away in Louisville. They helped enormously in guiding Dad to create the type of bourbon he had on his mind," Samuels Jr. said.

Marge Samuels was a chemist. She thought the best way to find the flavor grains that best complemented corn on the soft scale -- they had already decided that rye, which is the traditional formula for bourbon had to go -- was to bake bread with these other grains and see which ones are the softest. From that experiment and about

150 loaves, they decided red winter wheat should be the small grain, which would ride side saddle with corn.

In February 1954, Samuels Jr. missed the only day of school he missed through middle school and high school. It was for the first barrel produced of the new whiskey. Dad invited all the competitive distillers who were his best friends.

"It was cold," Bill Jr. recalled. "We had a little ceremony in the barrel room. We were leaving tradition behind and were going to reinvent a bourbon that actually tasted good, Dad said. That meant he was going to burn the old family recipe – It would have been his three great grandfather's" recipe. The Samuels have owned and managed bourbon distilleries in Kentucky since 1784.

"For the ceremony, he had a jug yeast bucket with a narrow opening at the top," Samuels Jr. recalled. He put the formula in with some other papers, spread some lighter fluid around. Just as he dropped the match, my sister put her face over it. It wasn't a bucket. It was a rocket nozzle. The result was it wasn't a flame. It was an explosion. The flame came up and singed my sister's hair. It was also the last time Dad tried to do a ceremony."

That got Maker's Mark started. The Russians were a few short years from shocking the world with Sputnik, and Bill Jr. and a couple of friends who were pretty good in math decided they wanted to help win the space race. For Bill Jr., that meant studying at Case Western University, one of the nation's great engineering schools, before going to work in California.

Red Wax

Meanwhile, Marge had decided Bill Sr.'s commercial instincts just weren't adequate. When he would come home for dinner after the second, third and fourth year, he would talk about how wonderfully the whiskey was maturing, how wonderfully it was developing. But in year five she never heard him talk about what he's going to call it, how he's going to sell it, how much he was going to charge.

So she kind of took over and figured the first thing she needed to do was to name the product and design the package. It took her three or four months. She had never designed a package before or since. Clearly her contribution has added almost as much as my Father's,' Bill Jr. says. Dad created what was on the inside, and mom created what was wrapped around it.

That iconic red wax came from the fact that the Samuels had about 18 old mid-19th Century cognac bottles that had been sealed to keep the air out. Marge Samuels was a fine pewter collector and was always in search of the "mark of the maker" on her collectibles. She thought the wax seal on the cognac bottles was a nice touch, and wondered if she could only make that functional cue a visual cue.

Being a chemist, she understood that she needed to back off some of the viscosity, and she needed to add some pigment so it had color rather than the dullness found in old sealing waxes from 150 years ago. She played with that in the Samuels' basement, and came up with what Maker's Mark has now. Bill Jr. has the first bottle at home, and, he said, it looks like what the brand is using today

From Rocket Scientist to Bourbon

Bill Jr. did rocket science for several years, but when one of his projects failed, he was terminated.

Dad wouldn't give him a job, so he went down to Vanderbilt Law School for three years and learned the business from Hap Motlow, Jack Daniel's great-grandnephew. Hap's father was Lem Motlow, whose name is still on the Jack Daniel's bottle. The Jack Daniel's corporate office was across the street from Vanderbilt Law School.

Hap and Bill Jr. would do something every Friday. At the end of those three years, Bill Jr. got really excited about the industry. He asked Dad if he could come back.

"He said he'd give it a try, and I told him I'd come back if he could see his way to looking at this as a business rather than a hobby," Bill Jr. recalled.

"I didn't quite know what to do. Dad's interest was in creating great whisky, not so much in the marketing side, so he left the outside work to me. My job was to go find customers. I did that for eight or nine years and didn't do much. I was about to give up and go practice law when we decided the problem was I didn't know how to do my job. That's when we hired an advertising agency. Not to do ads, but to teach me."

Chapter 2

A Front Page Article
In The Wall Street Journal
Leads to Explosive Growth

The major break occurred on Aug. 1, 1980. That's when *The Wall Street Journal* did a front-page center column feature on Bill Samuels Sr. and his little hobby.

That Journal article was an accident. "If you listen, you take advantage of unexpected things," Bill Jr. says.

David P. Garino, *The Wall Street Journal*'s reporter responsible for adult beverages, lived in St Louis. He was in Louisville for Humana Corp.'s annual meeting.

After the Humana Corp. meeting, he went back to the bar at the Brown Hotel. They had the news on, with a report about Maker's Mark Distillery being the first bourbon distillery to be designated a National Historic Landmark. Actually, it was the first operating beverage facility to become a National Historic Landmark.

The Journal reporter said, "Hey, this sounds interesting." The bartender knew who I was. They were able to get Bill Samuels Jr.'s phone

9

number. He was home.

The reporter said his airplane wasn't leaving until the afternoon of the next day, and if I had any time, he'd love to see the distillery.

Samuels said, "Great. I'll pick you up at 7 a.m. Then I had to call Dad, who didn't like the press and didn't like marketers. I had to tell my Dad I had a fraternity brother in town that wanted to see the distillery and really wanted to meet him.

"I knew Dad being a gentleman would put up with it, and then would "beat the hell out of me" after the guy was gone.

"That was one of only three interviews he did. He made only one speech, and I tricked him into that, too," Samuels recalled.

25,000 Letters

The moment that issue of the Journal arrived at the office, Dad said, "That's great."

And Bill Jr. said, "Yes. But it isn't over. It's just beginning." That was at 8 a.m. By 8:15 they had ordered five new phone lines, drafted his younger sisters and put them on the phones.

"Dad and I committed every night and weekend to personally responding to every letter we got. We had over 25,000 letters as a result of that WSJ article. We didn't keep count of the phone calls, but it was way up in the thousands," Bill Jr. recalled.

"That's when we said, 'Hey, we finally got

somebody interested in what we do, and we can talk back to them.'

"We took out our first ad – it was in the *Journal* -- and it was thanking folks for their interest in what we do in Loretto. We recognized they were going to have a horrible time finding it outside Kentucky. Just be patient, keep in touch and tell us where you like to have some." We kept the conversation going for six years until our expanded output was fully matured and ready for market."

It was the first time that father and son were fully aligned time on a commercial/marketing issue. "I had thought what you did was you went and got a bunch of sewing kits, put your logo on them and threw them around the bus station. I didn't understand what it took to get people engaged with what we were doing," Bill Jr. recalled.

"Dad never liked that approach. He always figured you talked to the people who were interested. They would then go influence and talk to their friends if they thought the product was worthy of recommendation and it would be the classic discovery model.

"Here we were, executing exactly what he wanted to happen. It was the most fun I've had in the business," Bill Jr. recalled.

Keeping Interest Alive

"Of course, we didn't have much distribution outside of Kentucky at the time. We were only selling around 80,000 thousand cases in total. We ramped up production at the distillery, but we knew it would be six years before we had enough bourbon to meet the demand.

"To keep interest in Maker's Mark alive during those six years, we begged and borrowed some bottles from Kentucky and sent them out to fine restaurants in places like New York, Washington, Atlanta. Not too much, just enough to keep interest up.

"By the time the distillery expansion was complete with mature whisky, the interest was still there. Ever since that Wall Street Journal article, the brand has averaged double-digit growth.

"I think if my Father, who died in 1992, were to come back and look around and see how well respected bourbon is, not only in the U.S. but internationally, what a fire storm bourbon has created in Europe, in Asia, he would be amazed . . . and proud."

Capturing the Dream

Bourbon's stature today just looked impossible back in 1953. Today, Maker's Mark has become an iconic product; and every distillery is sharing that success, and every distillery has at least one premium brand that is doing really, really well. "We like that," Bill Jr. said.

"Believe it or not, my objective has always been fairly simple...just don't screw the whisky up. If you asked me what I should have done better or different, I would have said: How come it took so long for me to understand how to take what was in my father's heart and translate it into a successful commercial activity?

"If it hadn't been for the work of the advertising agency guiding me, and teaching me my job while extracting from my father his vision and his dream, there probably wouldn't have been a Maker's Mark today and possibly there wouldn't have been a premium bourbon category.

"As I look back, that's the thing that embarrasses me the most – that it took so long to start listening to the man who created the product and to realize he also had a dream for the brand and for bourbon, and that dream was to move bourbon from 'kicking cowboys the Wild West and commodity' to the top shelf in fine watering holes around the world."

Getting Distributors

Samuels Jr. thinks that *Wall Street Journal* article might have been the breakthrough moment for bourbon because when Dad bought the Burks' distillery, bourbon distilleries were being shuttered about one every two or three weeks.

The *Wall Street Journal* story helped give people confidence they could carry the brand and it would be successful. "We didn't have many distributors or anyone who cared about Maker's outside Kentucky except perhaps 10 or 15 miles up and down the interstate highway. When that story hit, distributors from all over the country were making airplane reservations to come to Kentucky.

That was 1980. By about 1988, Jim Beam had the Small Batch Collection and Ancient Age launched Blanton's in the U.S. – great whiskies all. They were successful, and it started to give the industry a little gravitas. Samuels Jr. isn't sure how far they could have taken it by themselves. But the other companies jumped in, turned their master distillers loose and some great creativity came forward.

Chapter 3

A New Brand

For Samuels, after building the Maker's Mark brand, the next fun thing was creating Maker's 46, the distillery's first new product in five decades. "When we started we said this isn't going to be a gimmick. This isn't going to be something to go sell. We're not going to play with age and proof and that sort of thing. It actually has to taste good," Samuels recalls.

Bill Jr. huddled with Maker's Master Distiller, Kevin Smith, and said: "Kevin, what's the template? Let's see if we can mirror what Mom and Dad did when they got started." So they defined what success would look like from a taste profile or organoleptic perspective -- how an individual experiences Maker's Mark via the senses—not only taste but also sight, smell, and touch.

There was a flavor profile that they were trying to get to – rich, full-bodied, long, long finish and no bitter aftertaste. The goal was to create a big bold bourbon that had all the flavor on the front half of the tongue and surprised with a long bitter-free finish.

The longer bourbon stays in the barrel, the more tannic acids it pulls out, so you get a lot of flavor, but a lot of it is the back of the mouth where concentration of bitter taste buds are.

That's what they didn't want.

Barbequing Steaks Provides the Answer

They began to realize how hard it would be. Some PhD's working with them said it couldn't be done. But they kept at it. "We did 123 experiments, and eventually we realized we didn't know what we were doing, so we brought in the guy who makes our barrels and does all the flavor staves for the wine industry," Samuels said.

The barrel maker had a couple of PhD's in biology and chemistry. He said it would be difficult, but got working on it and stumbled into the solution one night when he was cooking steaks at home on the grill.

He was thinking about our project – how could he lock that tannic acid out and still release the sweet oak flavors, the caramels, the vanillins – when the thought occurred to him:

"Why don't I cook my barrel staves the same way I'm cooking my steaks right now -- Pittsburgh style. Why don't I sear the surface to lock in the acids, so that when the whisky hits the surface of the staves, it would have a hard time penetrating down to the tannic acids. So we would get more sweet oaks, and less tannic acids, which are congregated on the seared surface."

He went into his lab the next morning. It was a Sunday. He cranked the oven up and proceeded to blow it up. When he got the oven fixed, he said, "I've got something. I don't know if it's going to work, but conceptually we all agree it might work."

Samuels and Smith inserted those 10 seared, air-dried French oak staves in a barrel of Maker's Mark that was already six years old. And waited. They tested it every day for three months. After three months, it finally rounded up just about perfect. "I've never been so excited," Samuels recalled.

Chapter 4

How High Estate Taxes Led To New Owners

You'll often hear independent business owners -- those whose companies aren't listed on public stock exchanges -- along with farmers, ranchers and others complain about estate taxes.

It's not that they aren't willing to pay taxes. Any successful business owner views the government as his "partner." What sticks in their craw, however, is that estate taxes aren't related to income, but rather to the appraised value of a business or property.

They will tell you that they spend thousands of dollars to pay lawyers, financial planners and accountants to figure out how to keep their business in their family once they pass on. And then they usually spend tens of thousands if not hundreds of thousands every year to buy insurance so they can pay those estate taxes.

Failure to plan means the loss of the business. For a farmer or rancher, it can mean having to sell off a substantial portion of their land.

"Back in the old days, before 1980, Maker's Mark was a hobby," Bill Samuels recalled. "It didn't amount to anything. There was never any attempt at estate planning. Marge Samuels owned half and Bill Samuels Sr. owned half.

After that *Wall Street Journal* article, the value took off and Maker's Mark became a major part of their estate."

Simultaneous with that, Marge got deathly ill. This was before Ronald Reagan was able to secure the great reduction in estate taxes, when estate taxes were 90%. So Dad was going to have to give up the thing anyway.

So Dad and Bill Jr. went out and found a family company – Hiram Walker, owned by the Hatch family – to purchase the distillery and Bill Jr. stayed on. Six or seven years later, the Hatch Family sold to Allied, which became Allied Domecq.

In 2005, Allied Domeq was taken over by Pernod Ricard, the French distiller. As part of the deal, some brands -- including Maker's Mark, Canadian Club and Harveys Bristol Cream sherry -- were sold to Fortune Brands.

"We've had some very good corporate parents. Fortune Brands," now Beam Suntory Inc., "has respected not only the heritage we bring to the table, but I think a whole lot more – the art and craft, and how you have to treat it not as just a hard-nose commercial venture.

"That's not to say the performance has been bad, because we have had double-digit growth every year in an industry that's been growing 1-1/2 percent. The senior management in these companies has been very supportive, working with us," Samuels said, adding:

"I would challenge you to find anywhere else a parent company that has nurtured a little jewel as well as we've been nurtured."

Change of Command

The next example in guardianship occurred in 2011. Samuels says he didn't push for it, but senior management at Fortune Brands told him they thought the best successor was his son, Rob. "It really is amazing the amount of sensitivity, appreciation and respect they have for what we've been able to stumble into over all these years," Bill Jr. said.

"It really goes to the product. As we've grown, I've said our No. 1 objective isn't to grow but not to screw it up while we grow, because that's when it is easiest to screw things up.

"Unlike most Fathers and sons in this situation, Rob and I have almost identical personalities, so he and I can talk to each other without really talking to each other. Dad and I had to work at it, because he was the craftsman, and I was the 'out-of-control crazy'," Bill Jr. recalled.

Similar but not identical. Rob has a bit more common sense while Bill Jr. might be a little more creative, in Bill Jr.'s opinion. "Rob had the great good fortune of not working with his grandfather, but knowing his grandfather really, really well and spending a lot of time with him.

"He worked at the distillery while in school, and he did what I asked him to do after college:

Go be successful somewhere else. And he's been with me back here for seven years," says Bill Jr.

"I've told a lot of people that Rob in a lot of ways is really better than either his grandfather or me. So I think Maker's should be safe for another 25 years or so."

Chapter 5
How a Washington State Wine Lover and Chemist Came to Be in Charge of Production at Maker's Mark

It was a chance dinner at the friend of a friend's home that led Victoria MacRae to leave a job in San Francisco and take up residence in Kentucky, where she rose to become vice president of operations at Maker's Mark Distillery.

It turned out the dinner was at the home of Booker Noe, the legendary sixth-generation distiller of Jim Beam Bourbon, and his wife Annis in Bardstown. "In the 1980s, bourbon wasn't a big drink of choice on the West Coast. It was mostly wines, a few spirits. I really hadn't any idea about the history or heritage of bourbon," she told us.

"Over dinner Booker asked what I did. I was a research chemist by training, and at some point he asked if I'd ever thought about moving and working in the bourbon industry.

"My response was pretty much, 'No. I don't know anything about bourbon,' and he said, 'Well, you should think about it. And about making a move. I'd like to have more chemists

22

involved in the production process of our bourbon.'

"It really wasn't a conscious decision other than it sounded like a great opportunity. When I came out to Kentucky a few months later to talk with the team at the distillery, I was really impressed with the process of it, the heritage and the passion the people here in Kentucky seemed to have for the local product, which is bourbon."

After sinking her roots deep into the Kentucky Bourbon culture, she married Don Samuels, a distant cousin of Bill Samuels Jr.

Art, Science and Craft

People think making bourbon is as simple as distilling it, putting it in a barrel and waiting a few years. "But I learned at Beam and when Bill Samuels hired me to come to Maker's Mark there's a lot of art to making bourbon, but a lot of science and craft as well," she said.

In addition to Victoria, Maker's Mark has three chemists -- Diane Rogers, who is quality control manager and has been in the industry for more than 10 years, and two chemists reporting to her.

"It's finding the perfect balance between art, science and bringing all the handcrafted elements into play to be consistent with our founder's vision.. You have to have that balance and you have to have all three to make a consistent high quality product such as Maker's Mark."

For a chemist, what makes distilling different than other industries, we wondered.

"It's the inquisitiveness that people in science have about the product. So for me, my chemistry background helps me define an understanding of why the Samuels Family strain of yeast is so particular to our process . . . why is it that when we mash and ferment we get a very consistent product. . . . . What drives the consistency in the aging of that distillate because our distillate is very different from the distillates of the other products. Each of the other products' distillates are very different from one another.

"The beauty of a handcrafted product is you have differences but you maintain a quality and a consistency. Understanding the process can let you be more consistent throughout the process. I think I'm lucky to have a science background because I'm driven to get underneath and understand why things are the way they are. That doesn't mean we're driven to change anything but to get an understanding of the process and the crafting of a fine product."

Consistency Drives Sales

And it turns out there is a lot to learn. It's not just the red wax seal on every Maker's Mark bottle that drives sales. It's also the consistency of the experience for the consumer. That means looking at everything from the incoming grain to the barreling to the warehouse.

"We still rotate our barrels because that gives

you a greater consistency throughout the aging process. With a natural process you can gain some consistency and still have some variation that is totally acceptable to the process.

"It's the level of variation, of managing to a very specific taste profile that Bill Samuels Sr. created when he and Marge set out to create this wonderful product. She with the handcrafted packaging and he with the bourbon itself. He was very specific with what he wanted for the forward palate and how to handle the grains, how to use a roller mill, how to cook without a pressure cooker. All those things he understood intuitively, we're able to continue to do to keep that consistency of the product."

From Chemist to Plant Manager

Victoria had been in the industry for 20 years working as a research chemist, quality control manager, processing manager, distillery supervisor, and relief supervisor before Bill Samuels Jr. hired her. Bill brought her on board as director of operations overseeing bottling, warehousing and quality control in 2008. In 2010, she accepted the vp-operations position, which is effectively the plant manager. Adding to the production responsibilities, she's now also responsible for ensuring a visitor's expectations are exceeded.

How did she manage the transition from chemist to plant manager? We wondered.

"Well, it wasn't overnight," she laughed. As a

research chemist one of the things that really intrigued her was the process itself. "So I left the research lab and worked in the production area for 17 years, doing everything from learning about pumps and pipes to understanding the process and getting a deeper knowledge, whether it be filtering the finished product or distilling the new bourbon and the aging of it."

"One step at a time. Learn about the process. Take another step, learn something more. I may be doing what I'm doing as plant manager, but I'm learning every day. I don't think anybody ever stops learning."

Along the way, she learned about Kentucky, "what was valuable to the people in the industry, because they have such pride and passion in the products and where they live."

She oversees a team of 100 people, some of whom have been at Maker's Mark for 30 or 40 years. "It's a wonderfully effective team," she said, "able to respond to production changes." Some of the employees are second generation at Maker's Mark. "Each team member has pride and passion about our brand," she says.

In Hiring, Looking for Passion

In hiring, the first thing she looks for is "a passion for what they do, an interest in always learning, an interest in finding something they can be deeply committed to. Then I look at the skills. My tendencies always run toward meeting the person, the integrity, the interest the candidate has. If it's a highly technical position, we need to look at skill sets. But I really believe that the person with the right drive and motivation can learn and be a great fit."

We asked what she likes most about the job.

"Just coming into work. Every day is different, different challenges and successes with the team. The best part of my job is using what I know and what I've learned over the years -- be it from a process standpoint, a technical standpoint, a people standpoint -- to provide the team with what it needs to be successful. That gives me a lot of pleasure," she said.

The product " is a tremendous source of pride for all of us here at Maker's Mark," she said, adding: "If you look at the handcrafted package that Marge Samuels created, it's still very true to the original bottle. Then you tear that tear tape and pour that Maker's Mark into a glass. It's so consistent with Bill Sr.'s vision for the forward palate product that we have now.

"It's a good thing."

Victoria allowed that she enjoys the bourbon "on occasion." But she still drinks some wine. "Maker's and ginger ale is nice to enjoy at a family dinner," she said. And she enjoys grilling with the barrel staves. "Maker's 46 staves work wonderfully on a gas grill."

What a Tree Can Teach About Leadership

On the day we talked with her, things were

going well in the plant. Her challenge, it turned out, was a tree on the distillery's Great Lawn.

"The poor thing just struggles. All the other trees do very, very well, but we have one tree we have to take particular care of and it's just like every other facet of what I do here at Maker's Mark across the facility.

"Things work at different rates. People grow at different rates. The tree survives differently than the others, and the challenge is to have enough insight and foresight and to keep on learning things.   Then I can come back and provide the kind of leadership and guidance to the team and facility needed to sustain us."

Passion Key to Success

We asked what advice she might have for a young person. "It's all about the passion and the interest you have in what you do. If you don't have the interest and the passion, it's just a job. If you want just a job, that's fine, but you're only going to treat it like it's a job, and it's going to be something you can leave behind at the end of the day and on the weekends. That doesn't mean you're any less of a hard-working person.

"I don't give advice a lot because it tends to be one-sided, and people tend to hear your advice and think, 'That's what I should do.' But it may or may not apply in their situation. The one universal is you tend to become what you're passionate about.

"I have two daughters, and my message to

them is that it isn't about the degree you get, it's not about the field of study, it's not about those extrinsic influences. It's all about how you feel: Are you passionate? If it's part of what you are, then you'll become successful, and success will be measured by you."

Chapter 6

Catering to the National Appetite for Hard Drink

From humble beginnings in the last decades of the 18th century, distilling increased so rapidly, according to historian Thomas D. Clark, that "by the opening of the nineteenth century Kentucky whiskey had become a prime commodity in the growing western trade down the rivers."

According to historian Stephen A. Channing, for most of their history Americans have "had a prodigious and unquenchable yen for all forms of hard drink, and Kentuckians have been "quick to cater to the local and national appetite."

This thirst developed long before the settlement of Kentucky in the last three decades of the 18th century. The earliest colonists imported and consumed large quantities of alcoholic beverages, and almost from the beginning, they made beer and wines, using whatever raw materials were readily available.

By 1810 Kentucky's 2,000 distilleries had begun to challenge Pennsylvania for industry primacy and in the 1840 they surged past that State to take a lead which they have seldom relinquished. Presently, more than two-thirds of all American whiskey is manufactured in Kentucky, and the state produces 95% of the world's bourbon.

The development of a distilled spirits industry proceeded slowly, however, because most colonists lacked knowledge of distilling procedures and did not have the necessary equipment, and those that did had little time to put their expertise into practice because of the difficulties of frontier life.

Dutchman William Kieft is generally credited with establishing the first American distillery, on Staten Island in 1640, and many of the Virginia colonists are known to have distilled fruit brandy before 1650, but these operations were on a small scale and only of local significance.

Significant commercial distilling began in Boston in 1657 with the establishment of the first rum distillery. For well over a century New England rum was not only the favorite distilled beverage among the colonists but one of the foundations of the famed triangular trade of slaves, sugar and rum between Africa, the West Indies and New England.

In the latter years of the 17th century, alcoholic beverages distilled from grain began to appear on colonial tables. Within a century they would challenge and eventually greatly surpass rum in popularity.

The Pennsylvania Mennonites are believed to have distilled the first American whiskey in 1683. Whiskey manufacture received its greatest impetus, however, between 1716 and 1733 when large numbers of Irish and Scottish immigrants arrived.

Many of them had extensive experience in grain distilling in their respective countries. Most of these people settled in the frontier regions of Pennsylvania, Maryland, Virginia, and North Carolina with their portable pot stills and began distilling operations, chiefly utilizing rye or corn, or a mixture of both, for their mash.

In the last three decades of the 18th century, these Scotch and Irish pioneers and their descendants migrated to Kentucky in search of greater opportunities, and many lugged along their primitive distilling apparatus as well. Although Evan Williams of Louisville is often credited with establishing Kentucky's first distillery in 1783, indirect evidence indicates that others probably preceded him.

"What actually happened," says distilling industry historian Henry G. Crowgey "was that a people moved in who regarded liquor as a necessity of life. The distillation of liquor or brandy occupied the same place in their lives as did the making of soap, the grinding of grain in a rude hand mill, or the tanning of animal pelts," Crowgey said.

Thus, in its infancy, the Kentucky distilling industry was little more than a cottage industry producing liquor largely for home consumption with perhaps the surplus to be bartered for needed goods with some local merchant.

The signing of the Pinckney Treaty with

Spain in 1795 guaranteed American navigation of the Mississippi River, granted access to the port of New Orleans, and probably contributed more than any other single factor to transforming distilling into a major Kentucky industry.

The treaty gave the state's citizens an easy outlet for marketing their product. Because grain could be shipped cheaper in the form of alcohol and because demand for whiskey increased as the Nation's taste for rum declined, the output of Kentucky's distilleries became one of the major commodities in the downriver trade. Between 1792 and 1810, the number of distilleries in Kentucky increased to 2,000 from 500 and achieved an annual output of 2.2 million gallons.

Chapter 7

Before Maker's Mark, There Was Burks

The origins of Burks ' Distillery -- now the Maker's Mark Distillery -- can be traced back to this expansive phase when making liquor became more sophisticated, and distillers began to be specialized businessmen.

In 1805 Charles Burks obtained permission from the Washington County Court to dam Hardin Creek (in the present-day Marion County) for a grist mill he planned to build and operate.

By the end of the year, the mill had been placed in operation, and about that same time Burks opened a distillery to operate in conjunction with it. The distillery end of the business prospered and expanded. By the early 1830s, Burks' sons, Charles Jr. and Samuel, were assisting him in distilling operations which used at least three stills.

The early history of Burks' Distillery also closely coincides with the initial stages in developing bourbon whiskey. When Charles Burks first opened his distillery, he probably made whiskey or brandy out of whatever raw materials were readily available, and his products probably differed little from those in other States.

Within a few years, however, Burks, like most

distillers in Kentucky, discovered that whiskey made from a mash containing a large percentage of corn and a lesser percentage of smaller grains like rye suited the public taste better than straight corn, rye, or other combinations.

Also, Burks and his contemporaries discovered that the new stills and other equipment that became readily available in the early years of the 19th century let them produce not only a better quality whiskey but to adopt standardized manufacturing procedures.

In the early 1820's whiskey produced in the south central region of Kentucky, where Burks' Distillery is located, began to be called "Old Bourbon" in honor of the original Bourbon County, which at one time included 34 present-day Kentucky counties in whole or part. Soon the "Old" was dropped and the term "bourbon" was used by itself.

Although this whiskey was probably a higher quality distillate than any previously produced in the United States, it lacked the bouquet and reddish color as well as the smoothness produced by proper aging in charred oak cooperage.

Despite the growing demand for Kentucky bourbon, Burks Distillery encountered serious difficulties. In the spring of 1831 Charles Burks, Jr., died, and by the end of 1832 Charles, Sr., and Samuel had passed away as well, leaving Richard Burks as the only surviving male heir.

Richard, who had been in charge of the grist

mill, had never engaged in distilling, and there is no indication that he entered the trade at this time.

Sarah Burks inherited the distillery and a substantial portion of its equipment from her son, Charles, Jr., and that Nancy Burks purchased eight mash tubs at her late husband's estate sale. It appears, historians, say that these two women, who resided in the same household, probably intended to keep the distillery going.

There are no records to indicate whether they were successful or not, and in any case, Burks' Distillery probably ceased operations by the time of the Civil War.

In the late 1880's George R. Burks, the founder's great-grandson reopened the distillery in response to the Nation's almost insatiable taste for bourbon whiskey, which by this time had taken on most of its modern characteristics.

From 1889 to 1896, he and his father and brother operated the facility before leasing it to M.H. Chamberlain & Co, which apparently used the distillery until early in the 20th Century when George R. Burks took it over again.

In 1905, Burks took the lead in establishing the Burks' Spring Distilling Co. and sold equal partnerships in the operation to J.E. Bickett and J.H. Kearns.

With the arrival of Prohibition in 1919, Burks and Kearns sold their interest to Bickett, who apparently used the plant and its surrounding acreage for farming and livestock operations. In 1935, shortly after repeal, Bickett's son, Frank, and several associates began refurbishing the distillery and had it back in production by 1937.

In the early 1940s, they sold the plant to Arthur Cummins, who in turn transferred it to Ed Kaiser of Glenmore Distilleries. Before the end of the decade, Dave Karp bought the property, renamed it "Old Happy Hollow Distillery" and produced whiskey under the brand names of "Burk Springs," "Red Head" and "Kin Folk."

In June 1953, Karp sold the distillery and its surrounding acreage to T. William Samuels, scion of the only American family that has pursued a career of distilling whiskey continuously since the Revolution, (Prohibition excepted).

Chapter 8

A Distillery Farm
At the Turn of the 20th Century

If you visit the Maker's Mark Distillery, you'll be able to see the only remaining example of a typical distillery farm in Kentucky at the turn of the 20th Century.

The Maker's Mark Distillery, originally "Burks' Distillery," is near the heart of Kentucky's bourbon belt," nestled in a small valley, appropriately called "Happy Hollow," at the junction of Hardin's Creek and a narrow meandering stream or "branch," where it continues to make bourbon whiskey by the same painstaking methods utilized in the late 19th and early 20th century.

In addition to the buildings directly used to make whiskey, the site includes several nonindustrial structures which contribute to a visual understanding of life on a typical distillery farm in Kentucky at the turn of the century.

When Charles Burks began distilling operations around 1805 he probably used part of his grist mill as his distillery or else constructed a small attachment to it for that purpose. By the 1830's it is highly likely that the mill had been enlarged and other buildings erected to house the large amount of equipment Burks and his sons were utilizing in their distilling operations.

After their deaths in 1831-32 the distillery apparently was gradually phased out despite the efforts of Sarah and Nancy Burks to keep it in operation. The grist mill, however, remained in operation, and it probably used the old distilling structures to a limited extent for a number of years.

Burks Distillery as it appears today dates largely from the late 1880's when George R. Burks reopened it. At that time he enlarged and rebuilt the old distillery grist mill for his still house, and he probably added or refurbished a number of other buildings nearby as well.

An 1889 lien filed in the Marion County Courthouse indicates the existence then of the following present-day structures: Still House; Boiler Shop; Warehouse A; Office (at that time a barrel shed); Quart House; Distiller's House; and the Toll Gate House.

Toward the end of the century Burks erected Warehouse D, and in 1902 he built a house for himself on a knoll overlooking the distillery.

Apparently, no further expansion of the complex occurred until around 1935 when Frank Bickett and his associates refurbished the plant prior to reopening it after the hiatus of Prohibition.

At that time, a bottling house, a small warehouse, and a cistern room were added, and the Still House and Boiler Shop enlarged somewhat. Since T. William Samuels took over the complex in the early 1950's, the only addition to the core area of the plant has been a small wing to the rear of the bottling house. Samuels and his family are determined to maintain the turn-of-the-century appearance of the complex, and plant expansion has been kept away from the most historic area and is completely unobtrusive.

For over 150 years the words "Kentucky" and "bourbon whiskey" have been synonymous in the public mind. Burks' Distillery, whose origins extend back to 1805, is not only the oldest Kentucky distillery site still in use but the last extant operating example of the distillery farms that helped make bourbon, according to historian Gerald Carson, "the distinctive spirit of our country."

"Bourbon whiskey, for all the parochialism its name might imply," says distilling industry historian Henry G. Crowgey, "is most of all a distinctive national product, unique to its native land," a fact recognized by the U.S. Congress on May 4, 1964, in Senate Concurrent Resolution 19.

Burks' also represents the evolution of bourbon from a relatively crude beverage closely identified with the frontier into a quality distillate recognized and readily accepted all over the world.

When Charles Burks began distilling operations on the site in 1805 he made liquor from whatever grain or fruit was available, and his product probably differed little from that produced elsewhere.

Within a few years, however, Burks, like most distillers in this section of Kentucky, began making whiskey from a mixture of corn and smaller grains and installed more sophisticated equipment for its manufacture.

Although whiskey produced in the vicinity of Burks was called "bourbon" by the early 1820's, it "was not bourbon as defined today," says Carson, "since it lacked the bouquet and reddish color as well as the smoothness produced by proper aging in charred oak cooperage."

By the time George R. Burks, the founder's great-grandson, refurbished the distillery in 1889, in response to increased national demand for bourbon, these deficiencies had been overcome.

Chapter 9

What You'll See at Maker's Mark Distillery

Still House

This southward-facing, five-story edifice is of wood frame construction and is sheathed in brown-painted metal.

The historic still house rests on the same limestone block foundations that supported Burks' 1805 grist mill distillery, and its full basement and a substantial portion of the first floor area clearly predate the remodeling completed in 1889.

Windows are generally of the six-over-six wood sash variety and are set in rectangular surrounds. Red-painted wood shutters that grace the windows are of more recent origin.

The still house is capped with a gable roof covered with seamed tin and painted a darker shade of brown than the walls.

Like the older portion, it is of frame construction, clad in metal, and capped with a gable roof.

Inside, the building houses a 20-barrel-per-mash capacity distillery that is Kentucky's, and one of the Nation's, smallest legal distilling operations. Much of the interior woodwork is of

19th-century vintage. Particularly noteworthy in this regard are hand-hewn beams, joists, and hardwood floors in the basement and first-floor areas which probably date back to 1805.

Although most of the distilling equipment is relatively modern, there are some old items here as well. The basement contains a Gardner steam pump, believed to be 100 years old, and now utilized only as a standby power source.

In the first floor area are two copper Tail Boxes into which the whiskey flows as it comes off the still. These decorated boxes, made by hand, are sealed with locks which can be opened only by the resident government gauger. The building is in excellent condition and is well-maintained.

Warehouses

Warehouse A. This southward-facing, two-story structure is situated near the branch and faces Burks' Spring Road. It dates back to 1889, if not earlier, and is the oldest whiskey storage building in the distillery complex.

The metal-clad edifice is of wood frame construction, features projecting entrance towers at its north and south ends, and is capped with a low-pitched gable roof. Windows on the north and south ends are generally of the eight-over-eight wood sash variety, set in rectangular surrounds, and heavily barred. On the east and west side the only windows are at the second story level, where they are set in long narrow slits.

Originally the warehouse had a shed-roofed porch on its south end, but this feature was removed some years ago. Inside, barrels containing aging whiskey are lined up in "dunnage rails" at various levels which are reached by wood plank aisles.

Unlike whiskey warehouses constructed in recent years, this one features a central aisle with an outer row of barrels abutting the walls. The overall condition of the structure is very good, and it is well-maintained.

Warehouse D. This building, situated approximately 100 feet north of Warehouse A, is virtually identical to it in almost every respect. Erected sometime between 1889 and 1900, it features the same wood frame construction, brown-painted metal sheathing, projecting entrance towers at its north and south ends, and barred and narrow slitted windows as Warehouse A.

It is also capped with a low pitched gable roof. Unlike Warehouse A, however, Warehouse D still has its shed- roofed porch, which in 2012 was removed and replaced as a tasting room for visitors.

Located on the south end, the porch has been enclosed in recent years for other purposes, but it remains readily recognizable.

Inside, this warehouse follows a floor plan

similar to that of Warehouse A with its barrels lined up in dunnage rails reached by plank aisles. Like the earlier structure, it appears to be in very good condition, and is well-maintained.

Boiler House

About 50 feet northeast of the Still House, the two-story high Boiler House contains the equipment that supplies steam for the distilling process. Like so many distillery buildings, this one is of wood frame construction; is sheathed in dark-brown-painted metal; and is capped with a gable roof covered with seamed tin.

George R. Burks erected this structure sometime before 1889, and in the late 1930's it was enlarged somewhat to accommodate the bigger boilers installed after Repeal.

Office

The 1 1/2-story office, about 50 feet south of the Still House, was erected around 1889.

Originally part of the building was used as a rectifying room, and at a later date part was used for the construction of white oak barrels for aging bourbon whiskey. In recent years, the entire building has served as an office facility.

The structure consists of a rectangular shaped main block and a one-story, projecting, shed-roofed wing attached to the rear (west) facade. The edifice is of wood frame construction, is sheathed in brown-painted wooden clapboards, and is capped with an asphalt shingle covered gable roof.

Windows are of the six-over-six wood sash variety and are set in rectangular surrounds that are graced with red-painted wooden shutters of relatively recent vintage.

Inside, the edifice has been extensively altered over the years. Presently it houses offices, a large conference room, and a printing shop where the company produces the labels for its bottles. The building is in excellent condition and is well-maintained.

Distiller's House

This seven-room frame edifice, situated approximately 120 feet west of Warehouse A, was constructed in the mid 1840's to provide housing for the head distiller and his family. The structure consists of a two-story, rectangular-shaped main block, a smaller two-story wing attached on the west facade; and a one-story addition which projects from the north facade of the wing.

The house is of wood frame construction, is sheathed in red-painted wooden clapboards and is capped with a wood shingle-covered gable roof. A single rectangular-shaped red brick chimney with corbelled cap pierces the roof of the main block at its apex.

Windows. generally of the six over-six wood sash variety, are set in cream-painted rectangular surrounds, and feature wooden shutters in the same color.

For several years Maker's Mark Distillery has been carefully restoring both the exterior and interior of this house.

At present it is used as a reception center for visitors wishing to tour the distillery premises, and it contains exhibits of whiskey-making memorabilia. It is in excellent condition and is well-maintained.

Quart House

This small one-story building, about 60 feet south of Warehouse A, is probably the last standing distillery retail store in Kentucky and one of the few extant ones in the Nation.

Prior to Prohibition, many distillers in Kentucky and other States prepaid the taxes on barrels of whiskey for retail sale on the premises. Distillery visitors and people from the surrounding area would bring their jugs, quart jars, or other containers to a building such as this one where they probably purchased whiskey at bargain prices.

This building, which rests on unmortared limestone block foundations, is of wood frame construction; is sheathed in white-painted wooden clapboards with brown trim; and is capped with a wood shingle-covered gable roof. A single inside end chimney with corbelled cap pierces the roofline near the west end of the structure.

Windows are of the six-over-six wood sash variety, are set in brown-trimmed rectangular surrounds, and feature brown-painted wooden shutters. The entrance on the east end is marked by a small shed roof porch supported by carved wooden posts.

Inside, the edifice appears to have changed little since its erection before 1889. Presently it contains furnishings, ledgers, and bottles which appear to date from the early 1900s. The building is in excellent condition and well maintained.

Toll House

This tall, somewhat narrow building is about 300 feet southwest of the distillery's core area.

Originally it served as the residence for a toll gate keeper whom the Burks family employed to collect tolls on the road they constructed through the distillery property. In later years distillery employees probably lived here as well.

The house consists of a two-story, square-shaped main block and a one-story attached wing. The building is of wood frame construction; is sheathed in blue-painted wooden clapboards with white trim; and is capped with a wood shingle covered gable roof. A single red brick inside end chimney pierces the roof at its apex.

Windows, which are probably of the six-over-six wood sash variety, are set in rectangular surrounds and covered with red-painted wooden shutters. The front (southeast) entrance is marked by a shed roofed porch supported by carved wooden posts.

A toll gate with a stone-weighted balance, similar to those in use in the 19th century, has been reconstructed and is controlled by a rope from the front porch. The house appears to be in very good condition and is well-maintained. It currently houses a café for visitors to the distillery.

Burks House

George R. Burks erected a 2 1/2-story northward-facing dwelling, on a knoll overlooking the distillery complex, in 1902, shortly after M. H. Chamberlain Co.'s lease on the facility expired.

This irregularly shaped late Victorian structure is of wood frame construction, sheathed in wood clapboards and capped with a steeply pitched gabled roof covered with seamed tin.

Probably the most notable exterior feature is a one-story hipped roof veranda with decorative railings and carved support posts. It wraps around the front (north) facade and a portion of the east end.

Windows on the first two floors are generally of the one-over-one wood sash variety and are set in rectangular surrounds featuring architrave trim. Palladian windows are utilized on the upper half story.

Inside, the house seems to have undergone little major alteration over the years. The Samuels family has restored it, and presently uses it as a special meeting place for company business functions. The only major alteration has been the addition of a small, unobtrusive one-story meeting room at the rear.

Other Buildings

Included within the boundary of the historic district are several buildings of relatively more recent vintage.

They do not contribute to the district's national significance, but neither do they detract significantly from its late 19th and early 20th Century appearance. These buildings include the 1930s barrel house constructed of brown-painted concrete blocks about 50 feet east of Warehouse D; the metal clad bottling house erected around 1937 and located about 50 feet west of the Still House; the metal-clad cistern room which is also a 1930's addition and situated about 30 feet west of the office; three barns and a silo of uncertain vintage located on the south side of Burks Spring Road in close proximity to the Burks House; and a white frame tenant house located on the north side of Burks Spring Road about 650 feet west of the Toll House.

Finally, Burks' Distillery commemorates Kentucky's long time dominance of the Nation's $52 billion distilling industry.

Chapter 10

Where to Stay,
Where to Eat

Loretto, Ky., is known as the home of Maker's Mark. But the town was named for a Roman Catholic congregation of religious sisters founded there in 1812 to educate poor children on the frontier.

Loretto's population in the 2010 Census was just 713 persons who lived in 284 housing units. About 68% of the population has a high school diploma or higher, and the median household income is $33,333, according to the Census bureau.

Getting There: If you fly, the nearest major airport is Louisville, about 56 miles north of the town. It should take just a bit more than 1 hour to make the drive. Loretto is also just an hour from Mammoth Caves and Lexington.

Lodging: The Hill House B&B (110 Holy Cross Road, 877-280-2300) is the only B&B in Loretto, and it gets top reviews on TripAdvisor.com, offering a phenomenal breakfast and wine in the afternoon. The inn is a completely renovated farmhouse built around 1863 with all the modern touches.

Eating places in Loretto include Star Hill

Provisions, a newly expanded restaurant in the Distiller's House at the Maker's Mark Distillery which features farm-to-table dishes and seasonal cocktails, and the Cozy Corner Tavern.

Seven miles away, in Lebanon, Ky., a visitor will find the China King Buffet, Ragetti's Italian Food, the Cedarwood Restaurant, Henning's Restaurant, Captain D's, Lee's Famous Recipe Chicken and Stacy Ann's County Kitchen.

Missy's Out of the Way Café is 11 miles away in Raywick.

Of Note: Before or after visiting the Maker's Mark Distillery, you might want to visit the Oscar Getz Museum of Whiskey History in Spalding Hall at 114 N. Fifth St., Bardstown, Ky. (502-348-2999). It boasts a 50-year- collection of rare whiskey artifacts ranging from pre-colonial days to post-Prohibition days, including rare bottles, a moonshine still, advertising art, and novelty whiskey containers.

Spalding Hall was built in 1826, first as St. Joseph College & Seminary, then as a hospital that cared for Northern and Southern troops during the Civil War. Around the turn of the century is was an orphanage for boys run by the Sisters of Charity. The Xaverian Brothers ran a school for boys in Spaulding Hall from 1911-1968.

Photos

Bill Samuels Jr.

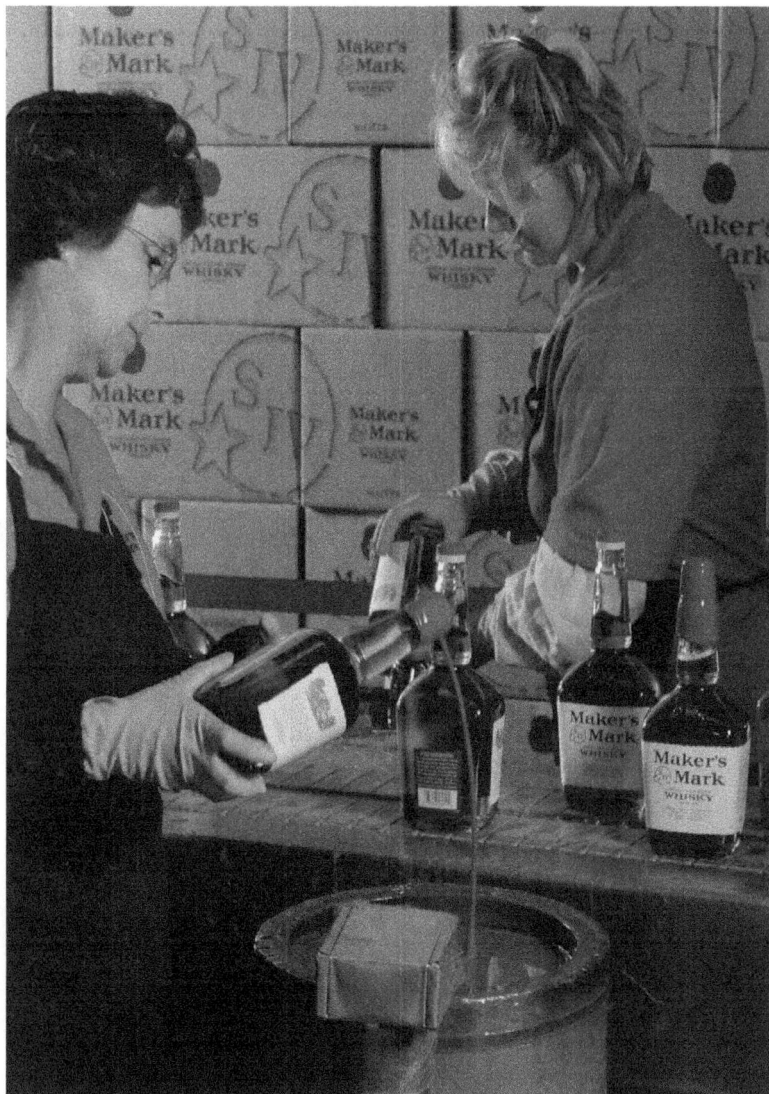

Hand Dipping

Inside the Maker's Mark Distillery

Maker's Mark Bottling Exterior

Maker's Mark Creek

The Distillery
58

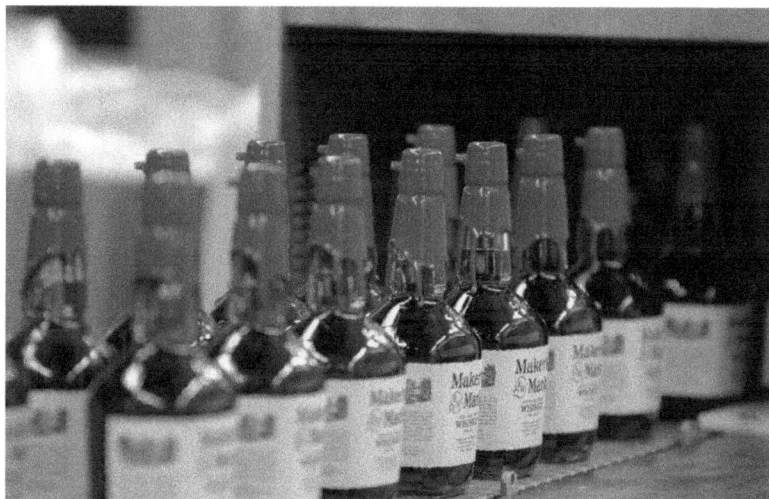

Bottles on Line

Inside a Maker's Mark Warehouse

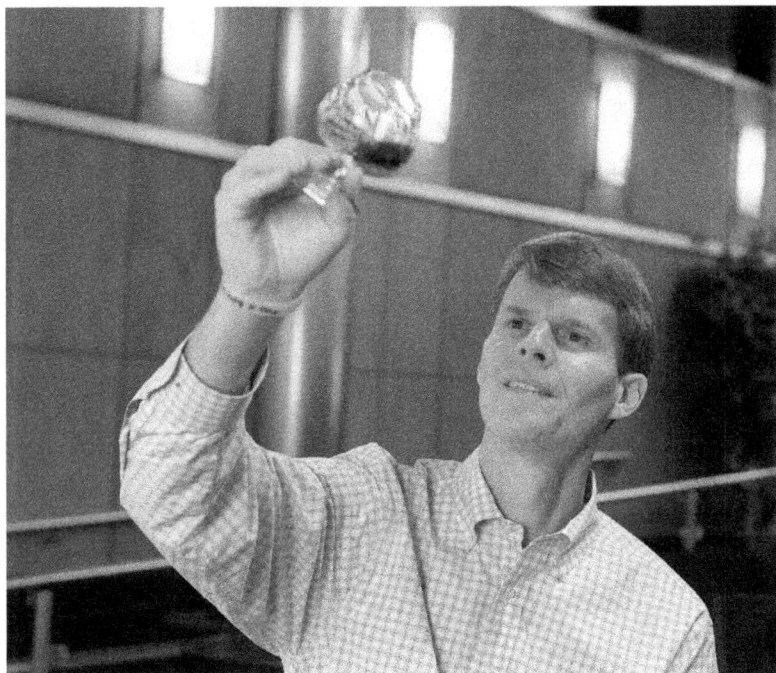

Rob Samuels, the new CEO, checks for color

Sour Mash

Victoria MacRae Samuels, Vice President for
Operations, Performs a Quality Check

Victoria MacRae Samuels, VP for Operations

The Maker's Mark Story

About the Author

Joel Whitaker was an experienced prize-winning newsman when he acquired "Frank Kane's Weekly Letter." He had been editor of the world's oldest high school daily and editor in chief of the Indiana Daily Student, the student newspaper at Indiana University. After graduating, he went to work at the St. Petersburg Times as a reporter, and later as an editorial writer and editor responsible for national news coverage.

He moved to New York in 1968, the same year Frank Kane died, as an editor at The Wall Street Journal, where he wrote the Page One news summary. In 1973, he was hired as business news editor at the Philadelphia Bulletin, then the nation's second-largest newspaper with a circulation exceeding 625,000. While in Philadelphia, Whitaker graduated from Temple University School of Law. After taking his bar exam, he joined the staff of Institutional Investor as managing editor of Bank Letter.

He bought "Frank Kane's Weekly Letter" in 1982, and has been writing it ever since. Over the past quarter century, he has broken a number of important stories. He beat all other reporters, including those at The Wall Street Journal, with the news the federal government would raise the federal excise tax on beer, wine and distilled spirits. He warned of the impact Mothers Against Drunk Driving would have on the alcohol beverage industry.

At a time when many industry leaders believed the alcohol beverage business was threatened with death, Whitaker accurately predicted the "French Paradox" would change the image of beer, wine and spirits to products which, when consumed in moderation, actually promote human health. And he was the first reporter to detail a pharmaceutical breakthrough – the development of a drug that has the potential for ending alcohol abuse, a drug that reduces the craving for alcohol experienced by alcoholics.

His reporting has been honored by the University of Missouri, New Jersey Chapter of the Society of Professional Journalists, and the Newsletter Publishers Association (now the Specialized Information Publishers Association).

He was Council President in Fanwood, New Jersey, a director and treasurer of the Newsletter Publishers Association and the Newsletter & Electronic Publishers Foundation. He's a member of the National Press Club, where he was Secretary for three years, and the Society of Professional Journalists.

Whitaker is an adjunct professor of communications at Prince George's Community College, where he incorporates stories about the beverage alcohol business into his Interpersonal

Communications and Introduction to Speech Communications classes.

Under Whitaker, Frank Kane's Weekly Letter was renamed "Kane's Beverage Week." In 2005, in response to requests for daily news updates, Whitaker launched "Beverage News Daily."

Today, top beverage executives receive a summary of the most important regulatory, financial, social policy and marketing developments news affecting the industry typically by 6:30 p.m. Sunday through Thursday, enabling them to prepare for the next business day.

Acknowledgements

This book would not be possible except for the interview Bill Samuels Jr. gave me. The interview was initially published in my subscription newsletter, Kane's Beverage News Daily.

Likewise, Victoria MacRae Samuels provided another wonderful interview, which is also incorporated into this book.

The history of Burks' Distillery, which was purchased by Bill Samuels Sr. to be the Maker's Mark Distillery, was adapted from the documentation submitted for the National Register of Historic Landmarks, as was the description of key buildings at the site.

Photos were supplied by Maker's Mark Distillery.

Paula Erickson, vp, global communications and public relations at Maker's Mark's parent company, Beam Inc. (now Beam Suntory), assisted in many ways to bringing this publication to its final form.

My wife, Donna Kay Whitaker, provided not only encouragement but proofread and formatted the book, speeding the publication process. Roger C. Parker, a book coach and proprietor of Published & Profitable provided constant encouragement.

Finally, this book wouldn't be possible without the subscribers to my newsletters, Kane's Beverage News Daily and Kane's Beverage Week. By buying and renewing their subscriptions faithfully, they have provided the economic support many authors get from publishers in the form of advances. They are all wonderful people who produce, market and distribute wonderful beverages.

Also by Joel Whitaker

This is the first in a series by Joel Whitaker of mini-books about distilleries on the Kentucky Bourbon Trail. To be notified when additional titles are available, please e-mail list@beveragebarons.com.

Joel Whitaker also produces a daily newsletter full of news about the beverage industry. To receive a free 15-day trial subscription to Kane's Beverage News Daily, please visit www.bevnewsonline.com.

To receive a sample of the weekly print newsletter, Kane's Beverage Week, which digests many of the Daily stories, please also e-mail subs@bevnewsonline.com.